Modern Industrial World

Spain

Neil Champion

Thomson Learning
New York

MODERN INDUSTRIAL WORLD

Australia

Canada

France

Germany

Japan

Portugal

Russia

South Africa

Spain

Sweden

Cover: Modern architecture surrounded by office buildings in the center of Madrid
Title page: A Spanish man walks through the whitewashed streets of a village near Granada.
Contents page: The Embalse de Riano hydroelectric dam. When the dam was built, the whole town of Riano had to move from the valley floor up to the mountainside.

First published in the
United States in 1996 by
Thomson Learning
New York, NY

First published in Great Britain in 1995 by
Wayland (Publishers) Ltd.

U.K. version copyright © 1995 Wayland (Publishers) Ltd.

U.S. version copyright © 1996 Thomson Learning

Library of Congress Cataloging-in-Publication Data
Champion, Neil.
  Spain / Neil Champion.
      p.   cm. —(Modern industrial world)
  Includes bibliographical references and index.
  ISBN 1-56847-434-2
  Summary: Surveys the geography, history, natural resources, peoples and cultures, and economy of Western Europe's second largest country.
  1. Spain—Juvenile literature. 2. Spain—Economic conditions—Juvenile literature. [1. Spain.] I. Title. II. Series.
DP17.C44   1996
946—dc20   95-33386

Printed in Italy

Contents

Spain Today

Spain is western Europe's second largest country in area, after France. It is a developed, industrial nation situated in the southwest corner of Europe. This area is known as the Iberian Peninsula and is separated from France by the Pyrenees. These mountains stretch for 270 miles, from the Atlantic Ocean in the west to the Mediterranean Sea in the east and reach over 11,000 feet in height. Spain shares the peninsula with Portugal, a country with which it has a lot in common. Spain also has the Balearic Islands in the Mediterranean, the Canary Islands off the Moroccan coast in the Atlantic, and Ceuta and Melilla, two small areas in northern Morocco.

Madrid, the Spanish capital, at night. This is one of the main roads in Madrid, called the Plaza de la Cibeles. The arch in the background is the Puerta de Alacala.

SPAIN AT A GLANCE

Population: 40,000,000 (1994 estimate)
Capital: Madrid (5,000,000), Europe's highest capital city (2,000 feet above sea level)
Main cities: Barcelona (4,600,000)
                Valencia (2,200,000)
                Seville (1,620,000)
                Alicante (1,300,000)
                Malaga (1,160,000)
Currency: Peseta (PTA)
Religion: Roman Catholic (50% of the population are practicing Catholics, but Spain has no official religion)
Languages: Castilian (the main language), Galician, Catalan, Basque (or Eusquera)
Birth rate: 1.3 children per couple on average
Unemployment: 24% of the workforce (1994)
Inflation: 4.8% (1994)
GDP: $488 billion (1994)
GDP per capita: $12,200 (1994)

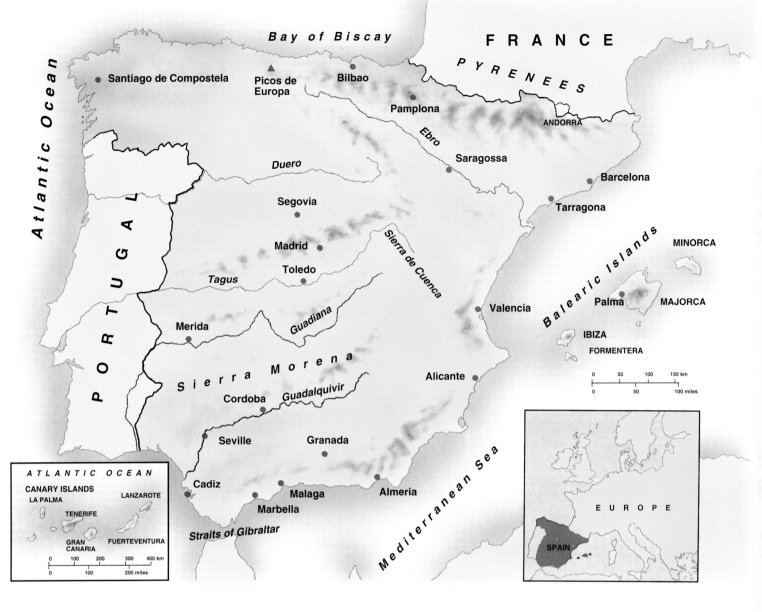

PAST AND PRESENT

Spain has many traditions that keep its past alive. Every town and village has its own church and main square, or Plaza Mayor, which acts as a focal point of the community. The Spanish still have a strong sense of community, and every evening people go to the main streets with their friends and family to walk up and down or sit at a bar discussing politics, sports, and their home lives.

A British traveler in Spain during the first half of the twentieth century noted that:
"Time was to show me that the lives of these people were so entirely bound up with their village that nothing that happened outside it…had any meaning for them."
– *Gerald Brenan*, **South from Granada**

THE MODERN WORLD

Television, radio, newspapers, and much more recently computers have changed Spain. Today, the remotest village is linked by these media to the rest of the world. Spain has moved on from its backward, agricultural past, although it has not forgotten it. Nowadays, it is a modern country, far from isolated or inward looking. For example, in 1992 alone, it hosted the Olympic Games in Barcelona; Madrid was nominated European City of Culture; and the World Expo was held in Seville. Spain has been a member of NATO since 1981 and of the European Union since 1986.

In sports, it has some of the world's finest soccer teams (in Real Madrid and F.C. Barcelona), and it is acknowledged as one of the best golfing nations, with Seve Ballesteros as one of its most talented players.

A farmer and his donkey cart in the square of a small village in central Spain. Some parts of rural Spain have looked like this for hundreds of years and today contrast with the modern cities.

Spain also has many famous monuments, buildings, and museums. Add to all this a landscape that is beautiful and rich in contrasts and a climate that is hot and sunny, and it is easy to understand why Spain is one of the most attractive countries in the world.

A folk group entertains café goers in Salamanca.

Spain has many rich cultural traditions on which it has drawn for musical inspiration. There is a Celtic strain in the folk music of Galicia, Gypsy passion in the flamenco of Andalucia, Latin American rhythm in salsa and rumba, and American and British influence in the rock bands of the big cities. A band called *Mecano* has become one of the most popular rock bands recently. Famous flamenco guitarists include Paco de Lucia, Tomatito, and Rafael Riqueni. They are accompanied by singers and dancers. Different cities and towns in the south of the country, as well as in Madrid itself, have their favorite clubs and flamenco artists. These are the distinctive sounds of Spain.

7

Historical Development

There are beautiful castles, from different periods of Spanish history, all over Spain. Some have been converted into places in which modern visitors can stay.

Modern Spain is made up of people with very different backgrounds and cultures. There is one dominant language, Castilian, which most people call Spanish, but three other languages as well—Galician, Catalan, and Basque. The varied landscape, too, has contributed to different communities growing up in different parts of the country. Spain is many different cultures all rolled up into one country.

KEY DATES — ANCIENT SPAIN	
3000 B.C.	The Iberians cross the Straits of Gibraltar from Africa into Spain.
1100 B.C.	Phoenician traders arrive. They set up a port at Cadiz.
900 B.C.	The Celts cross the Pyrenees from France.
800 B.C.	The Greeks start trading along the Spanish coast.
209 B.C.	The Romans start to colonize the peninsula. They stay for over 500 years.
A.D. 5th C	The Visigoths cross the Pyrenees.
A.D. 711	The Moors cross from North Africa. They stay for almost 800 years.

Spain today has a population of more than 40 million people. They have inherited the looks and cultures of the many ancient tribes and civilizations that colonized the Iberian Peninsula in the past. The invasions came from the north over the Pyrenees and from the south and east across the Mediterranean Sea. Spain lies at a crossroads, where Europe and Africa meet—the southern tip of Spain is only eight miles from the African coast—and where the Atlantic Ocean and the Mediterranean Sea merge. These factors have influenced the development of modern Spain.

No one can exactly date this cave painting, one of many at Altamira. The paintings are thought to be between 12,000 and 15,000 years old.

EARLIEST HUMAN REMAINS IN SPAIN

Weapons and bones dating back more than 500,000 years have been found near Madrid. Other evidence of prehistoric human activity has been found in caves near Altamira on the North Atlantic coast. Here, paintings of bison, stags, horses, and wild boar, thought to be at least 12,000 years old, decorate the walls of the caves.

The Iberians, whose name probably came from the Iberus River (now called the Ebro River), arrived from Africa about 3000 B.C. The Basques (found in the north of Spain) may be descended from the Iberians, but there is no definite proof of this. The Basque language is unlike any other language found in Europe today. The Iberians were skilled metalworkers and were the first to value gold as something precious.

Other Mediterranean nations came to trade with the Iberians. These included the Phoenicians and the Greeks, who built ports such as Cadiz. The Celts appeared from France, finding a way through and over the Pyrenees.

Descendants of this fair-skinned race can still be found in many parts of Spain, especially in the north.

THE ROMANS

The Romans did not come to trade; they came to colonize. This they did very successfully, remaining for over five hundred years. They shaped the society of early Spain and left lasting monuments, such as roads (which formed the basis for modern Spain's road system), bridges, villas, temples, and aqueducts at such places as Tarragona, Merida, Segobria, and Segovia. They also brought with them new agricultural produce and practices. Latin became the official language. Christianity was first brought to Spain in the first century A.D. Under the Romans, Spain became wealthy.

This aqueduct was built by the Romans when they occupied Spain 1,600 years ago. It is called the Puente del Diablo, which means "the Devil's bridge."

When their power declined in the fifth century A.D., the Romans were replaced by the Visigoths, a warlike tribe from central Europe. They made their capital at Toledo. They were blond and blue-eyed, and their descendants can still be recognized.

THE MOORS

Moorish influence in southern Spain is extensive and runs deep. The Moors came from North Africa in A.D. 711 and their last foothold (the kingdom of Granada) was not removed until 1492, almost eight hundred years later. During their stay, the Moors introduced new heights of civilization into Spanish society. More advanced in science, mathematics, astronomy, and navigation than any European nation, the Moors introduced beautiful new architecture; irrigation, which allowed more land to be cultivated; and advanced medical

10

After the Romans, the next major civilization to exist in Spain was Moorish (North African). This is the Court of the Myrtle Trees at the Alhambra, a Moorish palace in Granada, southern Spain.

Below *A statue of Columbus, who first brought news of the New World (North and South America) to Ferdinand and Isabella.*

techniques. Their religion was Islam, but they were usually tolerant of the Christians and Jews they conquered. Cordoba, their capital, had become the wealthiest city in western Europe by the tenth century. It had a population of 300,000, over 800 mosques, 700 public baths, and a library of 250,000 volumes.

THE UNIFICATION OF SPAIN

Spain was united into one country under King Ferdinand and Queen Isabella, in the late fifteenth century. Before this, Spain had been divided into a number of separate kingdoms. When the country was unified, the language of Castile, the most important kingdom in Spain at the time, became the dominant language. This was also the period of the Spanish Inquisition, when Jews and Moors were expelled from Spain and persecuted.

11

THE WEALTH OF THE NEW WORLD

Between 1503 and 1660, the amount of gold and silver in Europe tripled. This was due entirely to the Spanish and Portuguese mines in the New World. Between 1503 and 1510, 10,000 pounds of gold were shipped to Spain. By the 1550s, the amount of gold in Spain had risen to 90,000 pounds.

THE NEW WORLD

Ferdinand and Isabella also supported the voyages of discovery of Christopher Columbus. In 1492 he landed in the New World, the Americas, though at the time he thought it was India. The wealth in gold, silver, and land that this discovery led to was to make Spain the most important country in Europe in the sixteenth century. The Spanish monarchy became the richest in the world.

SPAIN IN THE TWENTIETH CENTURY

At the start of the twentieth century, Spain was mainly an agricultural country. More than 90 percent of the population were involved in food production, including fishing. Road networks were poorly developed, as were industry and commerce. Spain lagged behind most other European countries, except perhaps its neighbor Portugal, Ireland, and Greece. The population of the country was around 19 million. Most people were poorly educated, with their lives largely controlled by the church.

The victorious Nationalist army enters the capital city, Madrid, at the end of the Spanish Civil War.

CIVIL WAR

Throughout the early twentieth century, various groups organized, committed to improving the conditions of the ordinary Spanish people. Unions and other workers' organizations joined forces with political parties from the left-wing socialists, communists, and anarchists. This led to conflict with the right wing—landowners, nobles, industrialists, the military, and the church.

Elections in early 1936 put the socialists in power. But the army, supported by fascist governments in Italy and Germany, revolted. Spain slipped into civil war, which was to last three years and claim over half a million lives.

FRANCO

General Francisco Franco came to power during the war and remained in power until his death in 1975. The Franco government was supported by the army and the church. It crushed all opposition and silenced the press. Its policies cut Spain off from the rest of Europe for the next 40 years. Only when democracy returned in the 1970s, after Franco's death, did other countries really start to do business with Spain again.

General Franco, who for almost 40 years ruled Spain as a dictator.

THE SPANISH CIVIL WAR

The Spanish Civil War attracted attention from many young, idealistic socialists in Europe and America. British poets Stephen Spender and W. H. Auden became involved in the cause, as did American Ernest Hemingway, and a young British writer, George Orwell, who wrote a moving account of the struggle, the chaos, and the waste of life in *Homage to Catalonia*.

The Natural Environment

Left *Alora, an hour's train ride north of the Mediterranean coast, is a typical Andalucian hill town.*

The natural environment of Spain has influenced the development of the country over the centuries. The landscape and climate have determined the position and growth of towns as well as the agricultural life of the people. Environmental factors have also tended to isolate communities from each other, adding to the strong regional differences that are still found throughout the country.

THE LANDSCAPE

Spain has the second-highest average altitude (2,000 feet) in western Europe. The center of the country is dominated by a large plateau (the *meseta*), occupying about 80 percent of the country. This *meseta* is between 2,000 and 3,000 feet high, fiercely hot in summer and inhospitably bleak and cold in winter. The land is generally of poor quality, except where it is close to the rivers that cut through this upland.

Right *A sheltered valley in the Picos de Europa, one of two mountain ranges in northern Spain. The other is the Pyrenees, which lie on the border between Spain and France.*

LANDSCAPE FACTS

Longest mountain range: Pyrenees (270 miles long)

Highest mountain: Mulhacén, Sierra Nevada (11,407 feet)

Average height of land: 2,000 feet

Main rivers: Tagus (566 miles), Ebro (565 miles),
Duero (556 miles), Guadiana (515 miles), Guadalquivir (408 miles)
Of all the rivers, only the Ebro and the Guadalquivir are reliable
enough to be used for transportation and irrigation. The water
levels in the other rivers often fall dramatically in times of drought.

There are also many mountain ranges. These are found in the north (the Picos de Europa and the Pyrenees), the center (the Sierra de Cuenca), and the south (the Sierra Morena, the Sierras Beticas, and the Sierra Nevada). These mountains frequently reach 8,000 feet and often rise higher. They present formidable barriers to roads, railroads, and other communications.

Another geographical feature of Spain is the lack of water. For such a large country, there are few large rivers. This is especially noticeable inland, where farmers have always struggled to grow their crops. Over a thousand years ago, the Moors helped the situation by introducing irrigation techniques. They collected rainwater in cisterns and directed it through irrigation canals to their wheat, citrus fruits, and almond trees. This influence of the Moors is mostly seen in the south.

A worker in the front scoop of a tractor, ready to be lifted up to harvest almonds. Over the centuries, much of Spain's land has been cleared for agricultural use.

THE CLIMATE

The center of the country has a climate of extremes of heat and cold, which are intensified because the area is hundreds of miles from the sea. Any rain that falls occurs in the spring and autumn, but it is a dry region with frequent droughts.

AVERAGE TEMPERATURES (°F)			
	North	Center	South
January	57	48	63
May	68	70	73
July	77	88	84
September	75	77	84

RAINFALL AND SUNSHINE			
	Rainfall (inches)		Sunshine
	Max	Min	(hours per year)
North	53.7	38.3	1,880
Central	41.8	12.4	2,720
South	16.5	9.5	2,935

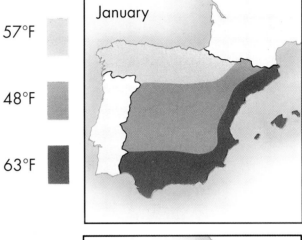

January
57°F
48°F
63°F

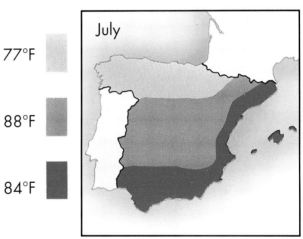

July
77°F
88°F
84°F

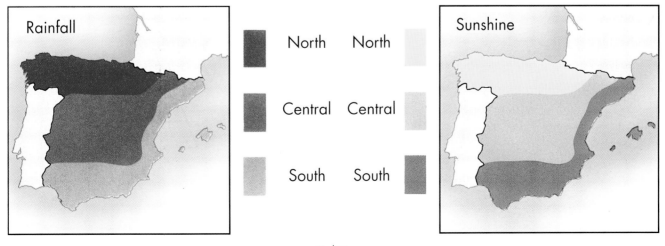

Rainfall

North North
Central Central
South South

Sunshine

The north of Spain is much wetter, cooler, and more mountainous than the rest of the country. Trees such as beech, oak, birch, and pine are common, and coastal valleys make fjords like those found in Norway. Dramatic cliffs and pounding waves make for a wild and sometimes hostile environment.

The south is warm and dry, influenced by the Mediterranean Sea. Tourists flock to the southern beaches, where the warm sea and sand provide an ideal vacation.

Spain's Wildlife

Along with a rich variety of landscape, Spain has a lot to offer the naturalist. Spain remains one of the least populated and most untouched of the western European countries. Its wildlife reflects this. There are still wild brown bears and wolves in the Pyrenees and Picos de Europa. Wild boar are still common in some mountain regions. The Egyptian mongoose lives along the hot southern fringes of the country, as does a type of chameleon. Spain is home to many rare birds, especially raptors. Eagles, hawks, and lammergeiers

Wild boar in Extremadura. There have always been boar in Spain's mountains, but like the bears that used to roam in the Pyrenees, they are becoming less common these days.

(a type of large vulture) can be found, though patience is needed to spot them.

18

The Regions of Spain

As Spain is a country that was united from separate kingdoms only five hundred years ago, each region today still has its own historical and cultural identity. Some regions even have their own languages. It is not really possible to understand modern Spain without some idea of where these regions are and what the regional differences mean.

A break in the cloud lights up an old church in Castile. This region lies at the heart of Spain.

THE MAIN REGIONS OF SPAIN (1991 GOVERNMENT STATISTICS)

Region	Population
1. Castile-Leon	2,563,000
2. Extremadura	1,057,000
3. Andalucia	7,041,000
4. Catalonia	6,116,000
5. Navarre and Aragon	1,745,000
6. Basque region	2,500,000
7. Cantabria and Asturias	1,629,000
8. Galicia	2,720,000
9. Murcia	1,060,000
10. Valencia	3,924,000
11. Castile-la Mancha	1,652,000
12. Madrid State	5,031,000

CASTILE-LEON

This is the land of castles—hence the name *Castile.* Most of the ten thousand castles in Spain are in this region. It is also home to Madrid and is the geographical center of the country. Its language, Castilian, is the language people mean when they say *Spanish*. General Franco insisted that everyone speak Castilian and punished those who did not. Over many years, Castile-Leon has come to dominate the rest of the country and unite it into the Spain we know today.

Castile-Leon covers 56,500 square miles (or one-fifth of the country), most of this on an upland plateau, the *meseta*. It is a harsh landscape at an altitude of 1,000 feet, with an extreme climate, but nevertheless the native scrub has been replaced over the years by wheat fields, vineyards, and olive groves. Many villages, though, have been deserted in recent history as young people have moved to the towns and cities to look for work.

EXTREMADURA

This region shares a border with Portugal, and in both countries there are plenty of cork oaks growing in the dry, unyielding landscape. Sheep and cattle have been raised here for generations. The soil is fertile where there is enough water.

Many of the Spanish who sailed to the New World in the fifteenth and sixteenth centuries came from this region. Those who returned used their great wealth to build large, beautiful homes and, as elsewhere in the country, to lavish gold on the church.

Goats straggle through a field of long grass in Extremadura.

Right *Gypsies dancing flamenco in Granada: there are many gypsies in southern Spain, especially around Granada.*

ANDALUCIA

This is the area of Spain that many outside visitors come to. It is home to some of the best-known cities in Spain (Seville, Cordoba, Malaga, Granada, and Cadiz) and contains some of the most popular coastal resorts (for example, Marbella and Almeria on the Costa del Sol). Tourism is the main source of income for the region.

The climate is the best in Spain: the summers are hot, the winters warm, and any extremes are modified by the Mediterranean Sea. Citrus fruits, almonds, figs, and grapes all grow well here. It is Spain's most populated region, with seven million people living in 34,740 square miles.

CATALONIA

Like Andalucia, Catalonia has grown wealthy from tourism. Its coastline includes the Costa Brava, one of the main resort areas in the country. The region covers 12,329 square miles and its capital is Barcelona, a city of more than 4.5 million people. Inland the soil is fertile, supporting large wheat fields, orchards, and vineyards.

The Plaza Cataluna in Barcelona, the capital of Catalonia. Barcelona hosted the Olympic Games in 1992.

The Catalan people have their own language, also called Catalan. They speak Spanish as well. They have a very strong regional identity of which they are proud. This was one of the first regions in Spain to develop industrially. Barcelona grew as a port in the nineteenth century, when it exported Catalan goods (such as textiles) to the rest of the world. Pablo Picasso and Salvador Dali, two of the twentieth century's most famous artists, came from this region.

NAVARRE AND ARAGON

These two small inland regions run up against the Pyrenees in the north. The people are more conservative than their coastal neighbors to the south. They are also poorer. There are many villages that are dying, with only the older generation left in the squares and cafés and in the fields tending their small farms. These regions are mountainous and wild, and they are being left behind by the rest of Spain. Only large towns and cities, such as Pamplona and Saragossa, get much attention.

Old men gathered in a village square in rural Spain

"The government is favoring Catalonia at our expense, just because of tourism. It is affecting our lives, as water is becoming scarce. It is as if the government does not care about us at all." – Irena de Vitoria, farmer's wife, Aragon

Water Wars

A well-kept golf course in Catalonia

Aragon and Catalonia are neighboring regions in eastern Spain. Catalonia has a long coastline on the Mediterranean and has benefited from 30 years of tourism. It is now a rich area, and the government has poured in resources to help development. There are many hotels, golf courses, water sports sites, and restaurants. The capital is Tarragona. Port Aventura, being built just outside Tarragona, will be Europe's second largest theme park after Disneyland in France.

Aragon, on the other hand, is inland and comparatively poor. It is farming country. The capital of Aragon is Saragossa, an ancient city built on the Ebro River.

The government has allowed precious water to be taken from Aragon to help with the annual influx of tourists to Catalonia. The water is used in the hotels and for maintaining facilities such as golf courses. It is also used in the industries that have sprung up along the coast. The people of Aragon are angry about this and have started to protest. But they are few, and the force of progress is against them. Today, many of the remote villages, inhabited only by the old, get their water delivered by tanker because they have no natural water left.

> *"I believe water has a social function. It belongs to the community. The local people should decide what to do with it."*
> **– Frederico Gonzales, olive farmer, Saragossa**

Sheep grazing on dry land in Aragon

23

THE BASQUE COUNTRY

The Basque people of northeast Spain have their own language, which is not related to any other in Europe. The Basques may be the descendants of the original inhabitants of the Iberian Peninsula. They are very proud of being different from other Spaniards and have a history of armed rebellion against the national government. Since the 1970s, terrorist attacks have been carried out by radical Basque groups. Much of the wealth of the region has traditionally come from heavy industry, such as iron ore mining and steel production.

Traditional costumes worn in the festival of San Fermin, in the Basque city of Pamplona in northern Spain

CANTABRIA AND ASTURIAS

These regions run along the northern coast of Spain, facing the Atlantic. They are separated inland from the *meseta* of

24

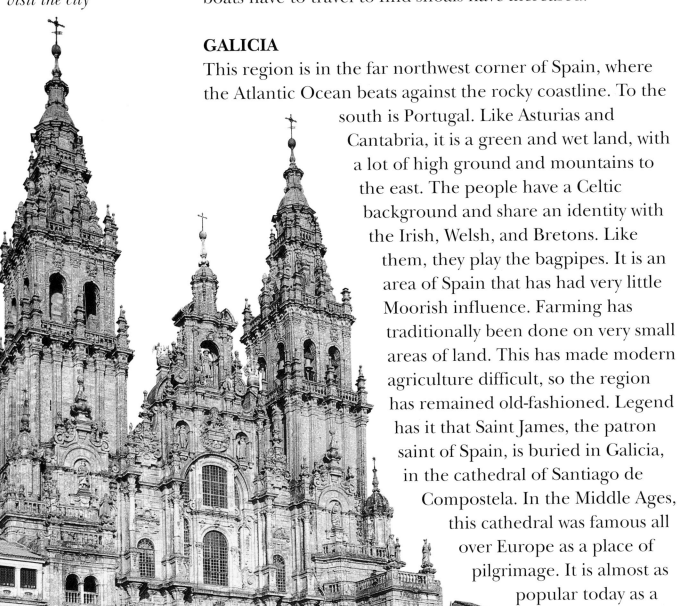

The famous cathedral at Santiago de Compostela, the end of a long trail for the Christian pilgrims who visit the city

Castile by high mountains, including the Picos de Europa. The landscape is green, due to higher than average rainfall. There is a lot of cattle and sheep farming. On the coast, fishing remains an important source of work for many men, although the fish stocks have dropped, and the distances the boats have to travel to find shoals have increased.

GALICIA

This region is in the far northwest corner of Spain, where the Atlantic Ocean beats against the rocky coastline. To the south is Portugal. Like Asturias and Cantabria, it is a green and wet land, with a lot of high ground and mountains to the east. The people have a Celtic background and share an identity with the Irish, Welsh, and Bretons. Like them, they play the bagpipes. It is an area of Spain that has had very little Moorish influence. Farming has traditionally been done on very small areas of land. This has made modern agriculture difficult, so the region has remained old-fashioned. Legend has it that Saint James, the patron saint of Spain, is buried in Galicia, in the cathedral of Santiago de Compostela. In the Middle Ages, this cathedral was famous all over Europe as a place of pilgrimage. It is almost as popular today as a tourist site.

Living in Spain

THE PEOPLE

Spain is a large country with a small population. There are vast areas of the country where nobody lives or farms. This is because most Spaniards today live in towns and cities. The Romans and the Moors started the urbanization process, but the twentieth century has seen more and more people leaving the countryside to look for work in big cities.

A busy street in Madrid. Today, most Spaniards live in towns or cities.

TRADITIONS

Bullfighting, guitar playing, and flamenco dancing are just some of the better-known aspects of life in Spain. The *siesta* is another. This is the midday nap people used to take to avoid the afternoon heat in the summer months. This habit does not fit very easily with the modern working lifestyle of the city dwellers. But long lunches are still the normal thing, and most office people work later in the evening than other Europeans.

Bullfighting — A Way of Life?

Bullfighting is a way of life in Spain. About 24,000 bulls are killed every year and 150,000 people earn their money in one way or another from the sport. It is still an important aspect of the tourist industry in many towns and cities, although there is a growing feeling that it should be stopped. The spectacle of a big bullfight is sought after by television companies, and today the top matadors are highly paid athletes.

"Bullfighting is a way of life for me. I cannot really explain how I feel about it. It is an art mixed with courage and honor. It is at the heart of our culture. The tradition goes back a long way and links us to our past. "
— *Juan Luis Barea, bullfighter*

Above *A bullfighter skillfully avoids the bull.*

RELIGION

The church still plays a major role in the lives of most people. About 50 percent of the population count themselves as practicing Catholics, which is a very high number compared to most other European countries. In the fifteenth and sixteenth centuries, the church became very wealthy, and gold and silver ornaments as well as great paintings of the period are still to be seen in churches everywhere. Almost every town and city has some of the splendid treasure that came from the New World centuries ago. Religious festivals and saints' day celebrations are big events in towns and villages all over the country. July 25 is a national holiday to celebrate St. James, the patron saint of Spain. Each town is also entitled to two holidays a year to commemorate local saints. There are so many of these throughout the year that the Spanish say there is never a day when all the country is working at the same time.

A worker cutting blocks at a small marble quarry

"I work, on average, 50 hours a week and the work can be very hard. But I suppose I'm lucky to have a job at all these days and to be able to do some of the things that I want. "
– Pablo Luciente, marble worker

STANDARDS OF LIVING

Along with other people in developed Western countries, most Spaniards want cars, televisions, washing machines, and other consumer goods. But the average worker in Spain still only earns 75 percent of the average wage in the European Union as a whole. Unemployment was very high in 1994, standing at 3 million people, or almost one in four of the workforce. Social benefits for those out of work are among the worst in the EU. Many people earn money on the "black" economy: working without paying tax, which is illegal, but widespread.

The Spanish economy has grown steadily since Spain joined the EU in 1986, and people have benefited in general. But the gap between rich and poor is growing. Those able to take advantage of opportunities in the improved economy have made money, but the need for traditional skills, such as farming and crafts, has been declining steadily. Office work in the service industries now employs more people than any other form of work.

WHERE PEOPLE WORK		
The working population in 1994		
Service industries (including tourism)	51.4%	(7 million people)
Industry	36.7%	(5 million people)
Construction	5.9%	(0.8 million people)
Agriculture and fishing	5.5%	(0.75 million people)

THE MEDIA IN SPAIN

After years of suppression by General Franco, the media in Spain is now flourishing. There are two nationwide TV channels: TVE 1 and TVE 2. These carry all the news and many soap operas, especially from North and South America. In the capital there is a local channel, called *Telemadrid*. But strong regional differences still play a big role in the lives of many people and generate a lot of TV and newspaper reporting. There are local regional TV stations in the Basque region and Catalonia, broadcasting in Castilian and the local language. On the national TVE 2 there is also a news program, *Eurodiario*, broadcast in Spanish, English, French, and German. Daily newspapers include *El Pais, ABC, El Mundo, El Sol,* and *El Independiente.*

THE ARTISTS OF SPAIN

This painting, The Parasol by Francisco Jose de Goya y Lucientes, known simply as Goya, is in the Prado, a famous museum in Madrid.

Spain has produced some of the world's greatest painters. Perhaps the most famous is Pablo Picasso (1881–1973). Others include El Greco (1541–1614), Diego Velazquez (1599–1660), Francisco Goya (1746–1828), Joan Miro (1893–1983), and Salvador Dali (1904–92).

Trade and Industry

These structures in Madrid are actually office buildings, with a modern sculpture in between.

POPULATION GROWTH	
(Year)	(Population)
1800	11.0 million
1900	18.6 million
1930	23.5 million
1975	35.0 million
1994	40.0 million

Spain has changed from an agricultural country into a modern industrial state in a remarkably short space of time. In 1910 about 66 percent of the workforce was employed in agriculture and fishing. Today the figure is 5.5 percent. In the 1930s, cereal products were worth five times the combined value of coal, iron, and steel products. In the 1950s, agricultural products accounted for only half of Spain's exports, and today the figure is even lower. People have moved from being farmers to being office workers. The service sector, trade, and industry have each grown dramatically at the expense of agriculture.

EXPORTS AND IMPORTS — DESTINATIONS AND SUPPLIERS		
1994 statistics		
	Exports to:	Imports from:
France	20%	17.5%
Germany	15%	14.0%
Italy	10%	9.0%
Great Britain	8%	7.0%

The biggest trade difference Spain has is with Japan. Spain imports four times the value of the goods it exports to Japan.

THE NINETEENTH CENTURY

Industry began to develop in the 1800s. An important iron and steel base grew up in the Basque region, with mining and processing taking place. Between 1875 and 1900, iron ore production increased by 700 percent. Most of the raw ore was sent to England for processing.

Centers of industry developed in places like Bilbao in the Basque region and Barcelona in Catalonia, bringing people from poor villages in as workers. As with the rest of Europe, the numbers of urban poor now began to increase. Famine and starvation still occurred in the rural districts when the harvest was poor (for example, in the period 1880—1882). But disease killed as many people in the cities when poor sanitation in overcrowded slums became a serious problem. In 1885 an outbreak of cholera killed 100,000 people, mostly town dwellers, in Spain.

COMMUNICATIONS DEVELOPMENT IN THE NINETEENTH CENTURY	
1848	The first railroad line is laid down. By 1865 there were 3,400 miles of track.
1849	Postal service is introduced.
1850	Telegraph is introduced to Madrid.
1880	There are more than 12,000 miles of road throughout the country.

The second-largest steelworks in Spain, in Bilbao. Since the nineteenth century, Bilbao has been one of Spain's main industrial centers.

SPAIN'S MAIN EXPORTS AND IMPORTS	
1994 statistics	
Main imports	Value in pesetas
Metals and minerals (including nuclear reactors):	1.5 trillion
Cars, tractors, motorcycles, etc.	1.3 trillion
Electrical goods:	824.0 billion
Photographic goods:	300.0 billion
Main exports	
Cars, tractors, motorcycles, etc.	1,700.0 billion
Metal products:	760.0 billion
Electrical goods:	500.0 billion

THE GROWTH OF INDUSTRY

After World War II, Spain was still cut off from the rest of Europe and from the United States because of its fascist dictatorship. However, by the 1950s, this position had relaxed a little. This was largely due to the fact that the United States saw Spain as an ally against Soviet communism. The year 1954 was a turning point. Spain received direct financial aid from the United States, Germany, France, Italy, and Great Britain, to build its industrial base. But this meant that as industry developed, profit often went out of the country. For example, the Spanish Seat car was built in Spain but under license from Italy's Fiat car company. Fiat earned money every time a Seat was sold. Medicines were licensed from German companies in a similar way.

Hotel building in the Canary Islands. During the 1960s and 1970s, the tourist industry in Spain expanded rapidly. New hotels went up in the tourist resorts on Spain's Mediterranean coast, as well as in the Canary Islands.

Heavy industry developed in Catalonia and Cantabria, where iron and steel were dominant. Large ports, such as Barcelona, expanded to be able to handle the increasing amount of exports from Spain's industries.

THE EUROPEAN UNION

A new phase of growth and development began when Spain joined the European Union in 1986. Today, 68.2 percent of the goods Spain produces are exported to other EU countries and 61 percent of its imports come from these countries.

Barcelona harbor: one of Spain's largest ports

33

Working in the Countryside

Small-scale farmers, such as this man, are increasingly rare in Spain today. Most farms are large and have modern machinery.

The old agricultural Spain of small family farms has nearly gone forever as rural areas have been depopulated. Today, modern agriculture is run like an industry. It has profits to aim for and markets to supply. At the beginning of this century, farms were inefficient, only producing roughly half the yield of France or Germany.

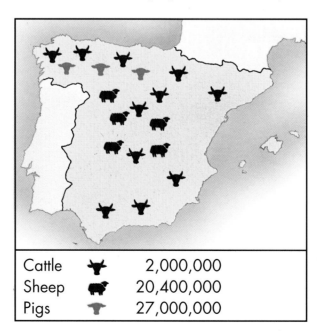

Cattle	2,000,000
Sheep	20,400,000
Pigs	27,000,000

MILK PRODUCTION

millions of gallons (1993 estimate)

Cows: 1,385
Sheep: 81
Goats: 73

Cows produce over nine times as much milk as sheep and goats combined.

People who grow food on small plots of land often sell any extra produce at market. Markets and stalls selling fruit and vegetables are a common sight in Spain.

Modern Spain has its future in the European Union. It has set its sights on supplying the markets of countries like Britain and Germany with salad and fruit products grown in market gardens. The Spanish produce oranges, lemons, herbs, lettuce, tomatoes, cucumbers, peppers, and onions, which can be found in supermarkets all over Europe. These crops are produced using the latest technology and make use of the intense Spanish sunshine. They tend to be expensive, but are welcome in the colder northern European countries, especially out of season.

Other important Spanish produce includes olives and olive oil, grapes—and the wines and sherries made from them—cereals (especially wheat), fish, and other seafood.

LAND UNDER CULTIVATION		
		acres (1990)
Cereal:	C	27,597,000
Olives:	O	5,239,000
Vines:	V	3,589,000
Fruit trees:	F	3,115,000

Market Gardening

"Spain used to be an agricultural country. It isn't any longer. It's changed in my lifetime. We still have peasants working the land, but when they die, their children won't take over their small farms. The type of farming I do is run as a business. I grow tomatoes and other market-garden fruit and vegetables for supermarkets in Europe. With modern transportation and refrigeration, the things I grow can be sold thousands of miles away and they are still fresh and delicious.

Fruit pickers on a large farm in Andalucia, with a factory looming behind them

This is the future of farming in Spain as I see it. We have to look for places where we can sell our produce in other countries, mainly the northern European countries. But we also have to find out what it is that people want to buy. This is the modern way of doing things."
– Alejandro Munoz, market gardener

Fishermen by their boat at Tarragona; fishing is an important industry in Spain.

THE FISHING INDUSTRY

The Spanish have always been big consumers of fish. There have always been fishing ports and fleets of ships on both the Atlantic and Mediterranean coasts. Today, Spain has to import a great deal of fish—over three times more than it exports—to satisfy the nation's appetite, because its ships cannot catch enough. The distances that larger ships travel to catch deep-sea fish, such as cod and halibut, have increased significantly as fish stocks have declined. In 1995, this led to a dispute with Canada over Spanish trawlers off the Newfoundland coast.

QUANTITIES OF FISH BOUGHT	
	tons per annum (1992)
Fresh and salt fish:	613,170
Frozen fish:	312,400
Farmed fish:	60,600

Tourism

A crowded beach at Benidorm, in southern Spain

Spain is one of the world's biggest tourist destinations. It has been attracting visitors on a large scale for about 35 years. Even under the repressive regime of Franco, people went to the Mediterranean beaches of the Costa Brava and the Costa del Sol.

TOURISM AND THE ECONOMY

The tourist industry has become an important part of Spain's economy. Today it accounts for 8 percent, which is about $40 billion, of the Gross Domestic Product, and is one of the most sophisticated and well-marketed tourist industries in the world. If you looked at this in terms of people's income, it would be about $1,000 per person. Tourism also employs a lot of people—2.2 million, or 16 percent of the working population.

This means that Spain is vulnerable to a large drop in income if tourists do not choose to come to the country. Spain is dependent on this fickle industry for a considerable percentage of its annual budget. During the recession of the early 1990s, the number of vacationers going to Spain declined. But the country provides bargains, and this has helped keep its tourist industry afloat in hard times. People still want a vacation, and visitors find a cheap destination attractive when they do not have much to spend.

TOURISTS AND WHERE THEY COME FROM	
1960	6 million visitors
1970	24 million visitors
1980	38 million visitors
1993	57 million visitors

86% of the total number come from other European Union countries. The main countries are (1993 estimates):

France:	21%	(12.0 million per year)
Portugal:	20%	(11.4 million per year)
Germany:	15%	(8.7 million per year)
Great Britain:	13%	(7.5 million per year)

The most visited place in Spain is the island of Majorca. August is the most popular month for tourists to visit Spain, with more than 10 million tourists arriving in the country. This means that, on average, every sixth person in that month is a visitor.

Vacationers enjoying water chutes at Ocean Park, Grand Canary

TOURIST FACILITIES

The government actively helps plan and develop new opportunities, although these are often in conflict with traditional lifestyles. Facilities designed and built especially for the visitor include hotels (there were over one million in 1993); water sport centers (more than 300 nationwide); tennis courts; golf courses (there are 136, which provide some of the most

Tourism in Majorca

The cathedral at Palma, in the Balearic Islands, looms over the town dock. The Balearics, in the Mediterranean, have some of Spain's most popular resorts.

Majorca attracts about three million tourists a year. The capital, Palma de Majorca, has an airport five miles to the east. There is also a busy ferry terminal. The island has hundreds of beaches and hotels, but it also has some spectacular and remote scenery, such as the Sierra de Tramuntana, a ridge that provides superb walking country for those who are tired of the beaches. The economy of the island has been completely changed by tourism. The small-scale agriculture of the nineteenth century has all but disappeared.

popular specialist holidays); spas and casinos. Spain's natural environment guarantees the sun and the sea. Its

"Famous people have been coming to this island for hundreds of years. They came for the solitude and the wonderful climate. Majorca has warm winters, and the sea is always there in the summer if you want to cool off. The writer Georges Sand and the composer Chopin came here in the nineteenth century. An English poet, Robert Graves, made his home in the village of Deia. He's buried there. In the 1960s, lots of young people from the rest of Europe came here to live simply and cheaply.

"Tourism really took off about 25 years ago. I've been living and working on the island since 1976. I opened a bar first of all. It did very well. It was close to the beach and the hotels. It was always packed in the summer. At first I didn't know how it would work out in the winter, but there were still lots of tourists around. They tended to be older than the summer ones. They were retired and richer. This meant that my business could be kept going all year round and this made a big difference. After five years I had made enough money to be able to open a small hotel.

"The tourist trade has remained good to the island in spite of the recession. People still seem to be able to afford to come here."
– *Luis Torres, hotel and bar owner*

Selling trinkets on the roadside. Stalls, such as this one in Majorca, are common in tourist areas.

mountains offer excellent walking terrain, with skiing in the winter in the Sierra Nevada and Pyrenees.

THE BALEARIC ISLANDS

Ciudadela harbor, in Minorca, is a popular stopping place for sailors on a visit to the Balearic Islands.

The Balearic Islands are many people's idea of an ideal vacation destination: miles of beaches, fashionable bars, ancient monuments, hot summers, and mild winters. The four islands are found about 125 miles off the coast of Spain in the Mediterranean Sea. Majorca (1,405 square miles) is the largest: its capital is Palma. The other three are Minorca, Ibiza, and Formentera. They have around 710,000 inhabitants. The islands were recaptured from the Moors in 1229 and came under the rule of Catalonia. Catalan, the Catalonian language, is still spoken.

Many nineteenth-century writers, artists, and composers discovered the beauty of the Balearic Islands. In the middle of the century, Frédéric Chopin wrote:
"I am now in Palma amidst palm trees, cedars, aloes, orange trees, lemon trees, fig trees, and pomegranates. The sky is turquoise, the sea is blue, and the mountains are emerald...the sun shines all day....In a word, life here is delicious."
– Frédéric Chopin, composer

CULTURAL HERITAGE

The cultural history of Spain is diverse and attractive to the tourist. The artistic and architectural remains of the invading nations of the past are very much in evidence around the country, especially those of the Romans, the Moors, and the Christian kingdoms of the fifteenth and sixteenth centuries. Spain's cultural heritage includes about ten thousand castles and other monuments and over three hundred historical sites of importance. The Romans left aqueducts, mosaics, temples, and amphitheaters; the Moors built Granada, one of the most beautiful cities in the world, as well as many great mosques and public buildings. About an hour away from Madrid, in the foothills of the Guadarrama Mountains, lies El Escorial, the monastery-palace of Philip II, built in 1584. This has been called the eighth wonder of the world and ranks as one of the great Renaissance monuments. All these sights attract many thousands of tourists every year.

This Roman theater at Merida, in southern Spain, was built in 24 B.C. It attracts thousands of visitors every year.

Spain's Future

Spain has come a long way since joining the European Union. But many of the benefits of economic growth in the late 1980s and early 1990s have disappeared in the recession. Spain, like many other countries around the world, is recovering from the effects of this recession. It is doing so by concentrating on exports. To succeed, Spanish industries must keep prices down so that Spain can compete with the exports of other countries on the world market. One way of doing this is to keep wages as low as possible. Another way is to use as few people as possible to get a job done. Both these things imply hard times for the working people of the country. This is shown in some of the national statistics. In 1994, Spain had one of the highest unemployment rates in the EU at 24 percent, and wages were below the average. Benefits for the unemployed or low paid workers were among the worst in the Union.

A great deal of modern Spanish industry is owned by companies from other countries. For a decade, the Spanish government has followed a policy that has attracted foreign investment. This has come not only from car manufacturers such as Fiat, but also from electronics companies and the pharmaceutical industry. But there is a price to pay, and that price is the profit. Most of this goes to the multinational companies, which have had good tax incentives from the Spanish government. Relatively little money, apart from that

Spaniards sitting in the open air, outside a cafe in Madrid

paid in wages to the Spanish workers, finds its way back into the Spanish economy.

These are significant problems that face the government of the country. On the positive side, tourism continues to boom, and market-garden produce, along with Spanish regional wine, continues to sell well in the EU.

Since joining the European Union, Spain has committed itself wholeheartedly to its progress and is aiming to join the single currency of Europe when this comes about. But the people of Spain are still waiting for an upturn in their living standards after the recession. There is need for rural regeneration across the country and investment in the inner cities. These things, combined with the need for more investment in social welfare to bring Spain into line with the EU, will put a great deal of financial pressure on the government today and in the future.

A Student's View

"I spent three months learning English in England. I had a good time. I was in Canterbury. There were many students from other countries. This was in 1993. An experience like that makes you feel part of the EU, part of the future of Europe. I studied business in Madrid, and I'm trying to get work in a publishing company here or abroad. Education is important, and it leads to the wider world where travel and living abroad are part of what you do. Spain wants to make the EU work and there are opportunities for people like me, people who have grown up with pop music and computers and television, which never existed for our parents."

– *Esther Duarte, student, Madrid*

Glossary

"Black" economy Money earned unofficially by people to avoid paying taxes to the government.

Communism A political theory that says that private property is wrong and that the people should own all the means by which money is made, including industry, banks, agriculture, and transportation. In practice, Communist governments have usually been dictatorships.

Democracy A political system in which the people elect a government to run the country on their behalf.

Descendant A person who can trace (through parents, grandparents, great grandparents, and so on) his or her origins back to another person or group of people from the past.

Dictator A person who rules over a country and its people, usually without asking their opinion about how the country should be run.

European Union A group of European countries that have agreed to have free trade among themselves and to have certain laws in common. These countries are Austria, Belgium, Denmark, France, Germany, Greece, Ireland, Italy, Luxembourg, the Netherlands, Portugal, Spain, and Great Britain. Other countries are waiting to join.

Exports The products made in a country and sold abroad.

Fascism A political movement that is based on military ideals and nationalism. Germany under Hitler and Italy under Mussolini are two twentieth-century examples of fascist governments.

Gross Domestic Product (GDP) The total amount of goods and services produced by a country in any one year.

Heavy industry Basic types of industry, such as shipbuilding, machinemaking, mining, and steel producing.

Imports Products that are bought from abroad.

Inflation The increase in prices of goods and services that happens over a period of time.

Meseta The dry plateau found in the center of Spain.

Moors The Arab and Berber conquerors of Spain. This term was used by the Spanish to describe all Muslims in Spain.

NATO The North Atlantic Treaty Organization. An alliance that links the United States and Canada to a group of European States to deal with defense matters.

Pharmaceutical industry The industry that produces medicines and the chemicals that are used make medicines.

Radical A person or belief that is politically extreme.

Raptor A seldom used general word for birds of prey. Raptors include falcons, eagles, hawks, and vultures.

Service industry The industry that looks after the needs of others, for example, hotels, transportation, and leisure complexes, but that does not produce anything itself.

Socialism An intermediate political system between Communism and Capitalism, in which many industries and properties are controlled by the government, but wealth is not distributed equally among the people.

Urbanization The movement of people to towns, often because there is no work in the countryside.

Further Information

BOOKS

Bachrach, Deborah. *Inquisition*. World History. San Diego: Lucent Books, 1994.

Chrisp, Peter. *Spanish Conquests in the New World*. Exploration and Encounters. New York: Thomson Learning, 1993.

Garza, Hedda. *Francisco Franco*. World Leaders: Past & Present. New York: Chelsea House, 1987.

Goodwin, Bob and Perez, Candi. *A Taste of Spain*. Food Around the World. New York: Thomson Learning, 1995.

Leahy, Philippa. *Spain*. Discovering. New York: Crestwood House, 1995.

Miller, Arthur. *Spain*. Let's Visit Places and Peoples of the World. New York: Chelsea House, 1989.

Stevens, Paul. *Ferdinand and Isabella*. World Leaders: Past & Present. New York: Chelsea House, 1988.

Literature about Spain by English-speaking authors include the following:
Homage to Catalonia (1938) by George Orwell.
Death in the Afternoon (1932) and *For Whom the Bell Tolls* (1940) by Ernest Hemingway..

INFORMATION

You can write to these offices for more information on Spain:

The Spanish Embassy
2700 15th Street NW
Washington, DC 20009
Tel: (202) 265-0190

Spanish National Tourism Office
665 Fifth Avenue
New York, NY 10022
Tel: (212) 759-8822

All the boxed information in the text has been provided by the Information Counselor at the Spanish Embassy in London, England.

PICTURE ACKNOWLEDGMENTS
Grateful thanks to the following for allowing their photographs to be reproduced in this book:
Ancient Art and Architecture Collection: 9; The Bridgeman Art Library: 29; Camera Press Ltd.: 13 (Gyenes), 24 (Blanca Castillo), 41 (Haydn Jones); J. Allan Cash Photo Library: 20, 42; Cephas Picture Library: 6 (Mick Rock), 22 top (Peter Stowell); The Mary Evans Picture Library: 12; Eye Ubiquitous: *title page*, 11 bottom, 23 top, 25, 26, 33, 35, and 40 (James Davis), 11 top, 31, and 38 (David Cumming), 32 and 39 (Paul Thompson), 28 (Mike Feeney), and *cover*; Medimage: contents page, 7, 10, 15, 16, 22 bottom, 30, and 37 (Anthony King); Oxford Scientific Films: 18 (Richard and Julia Kemp); Tony Stone Worldwide: 4 and 44 (Doug Armand), 14 (Chris Haigh), 21 right (Robert Everts), 27 (Florence Douyrou), 36 (Robert Frerck); Topham Picture Source: 23 bottom, 34, 43; WPL: 45.
Maps on pages 5, 17, 19, 34, and 35 were provided by Peter Bull.

Index

The figures in **bold** refer to photographs and maps.